Let's Count All the Animals!

by Jim E. Kulas
pictures by Terry Wickart

A GOLDEN BOOK • NEW YORK
Western Publishing Company, Inc.
Racine, Wisconsin 53404

We'll visit a farm,
And we'll visit the zoo.
We'll have some fun counting,
So won't you come, too?

1 One jumping dog barks after us.
He wants to come and makes a fuss.

2 Two quick brown cats run down the street.
They smell some fish they'd like to eat.

3 First stop—the zoo! See, big and strong,
Three elephants with trunks so long.

4 What have small ears, and short legs, too?
Four hippopotamuses do!

5 There, bending low and standing tall,
The five giraffes make us feel small.

6 Six lions—count them while they play
And chase and jump and sleep today.

7 These seven penguins look polite
In party suits of black and white.

8 Eight monkeys frolic on their hill.
They scurry round—not one is still.

9 Not far away, nine gentle deer
Will stay if we are still when near.

10 Ten sleepy turtles nap or crawl.
Some hardly show their heads at all.

11 Eleven fish, in water bright,
Have many colors, dark and light.

12 We leave the zoo, and wave good-bye
To twelve goats climbing up, up high.

13 Next stop—a farm! What do we see?
Thirteen horses grazing free.

14 Fourteen cows! Some say, "Moo, moo."
Perhaps it means, "Well, how are you?"

15 Fifteen pigs, sleek, in a row,
Say, "Oink! We're hungry. Don't you know?"

16 Sixteen rabbits near their hutch!
They like fresh carrots very much.

17 Seventeen chickens near their coops—
Some cluck, some run, some peck in groups.

18 Eighteen field mice run to hide,
Both *on* the ground, and deep *inside!*

19 Nineteen sheep say, "Baa." We say, "Good-bye! We'll come again someday."